Twenty progressive exercises for the violin, with accompaniment of a second violin. [Op. 38]

Jakob Dont

SCHIRMER'S
LIBRARY

Vol. 429

DONT

TWENTY
PROGRESSIVE
EXERCISES

FOR

VIOLIN

Op. 38

Pr., 75c.

Schirmer's Library of Musical Classics

Vol. 429

JACQUES DONT

Op. 38

TWENTY
PROGRESSIVE
EXERCISES

FOR THE

VIOLIN

WITH ACCOMPANIMENT OF A
SECOND VIOLIN

G. SCHIRMER, INC., NEW YORK

1897

Printed in the U.S.A.

Twenty
Progressive Exercises
for
Two Violins.

∧ Up-bow.

⊔ Down-bow.

JAC. DONT. Op. 38.

13243

*) With strongly marked, detached bows at the point or the middle.

4

Allegro moderato.

4.

8

Allegro moderato.

5.

Allegretto.

6.

Allegro non troppo.

8.

f ben legato

cantabile

16

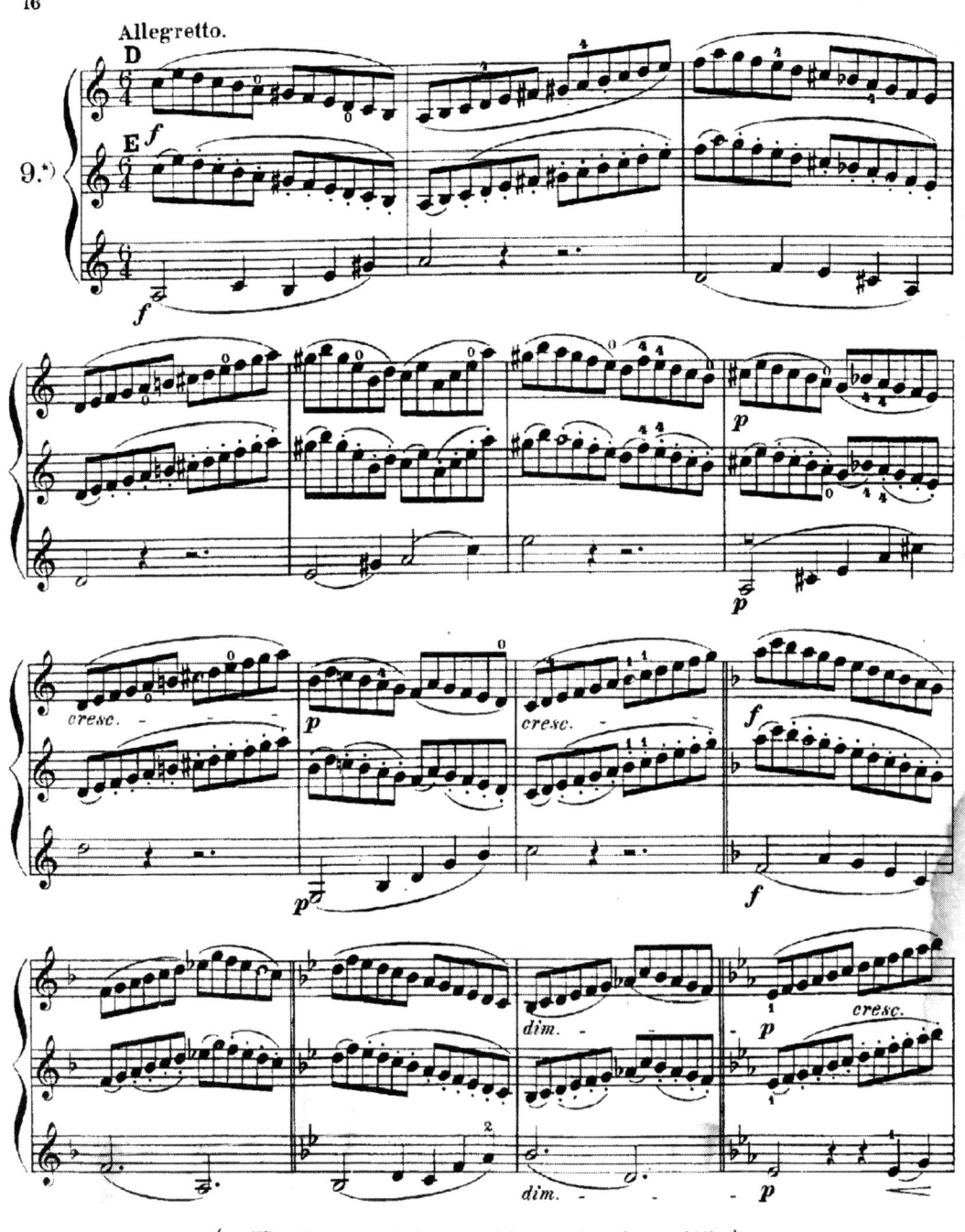

A. With strongly marked, detached bows at the point or middle.
B. With legato (smooth) detached bows at the point or the middle.
C. With springing bow (spiccato)..
D & E. See the above two lines marked with these letters............

The Tempo may be taken quick or slow at pleasure.

13248

Andante, quasi Allegretto.

10.

13248

Allegro moderato.

13.

28

Allegro appassionato.

14.

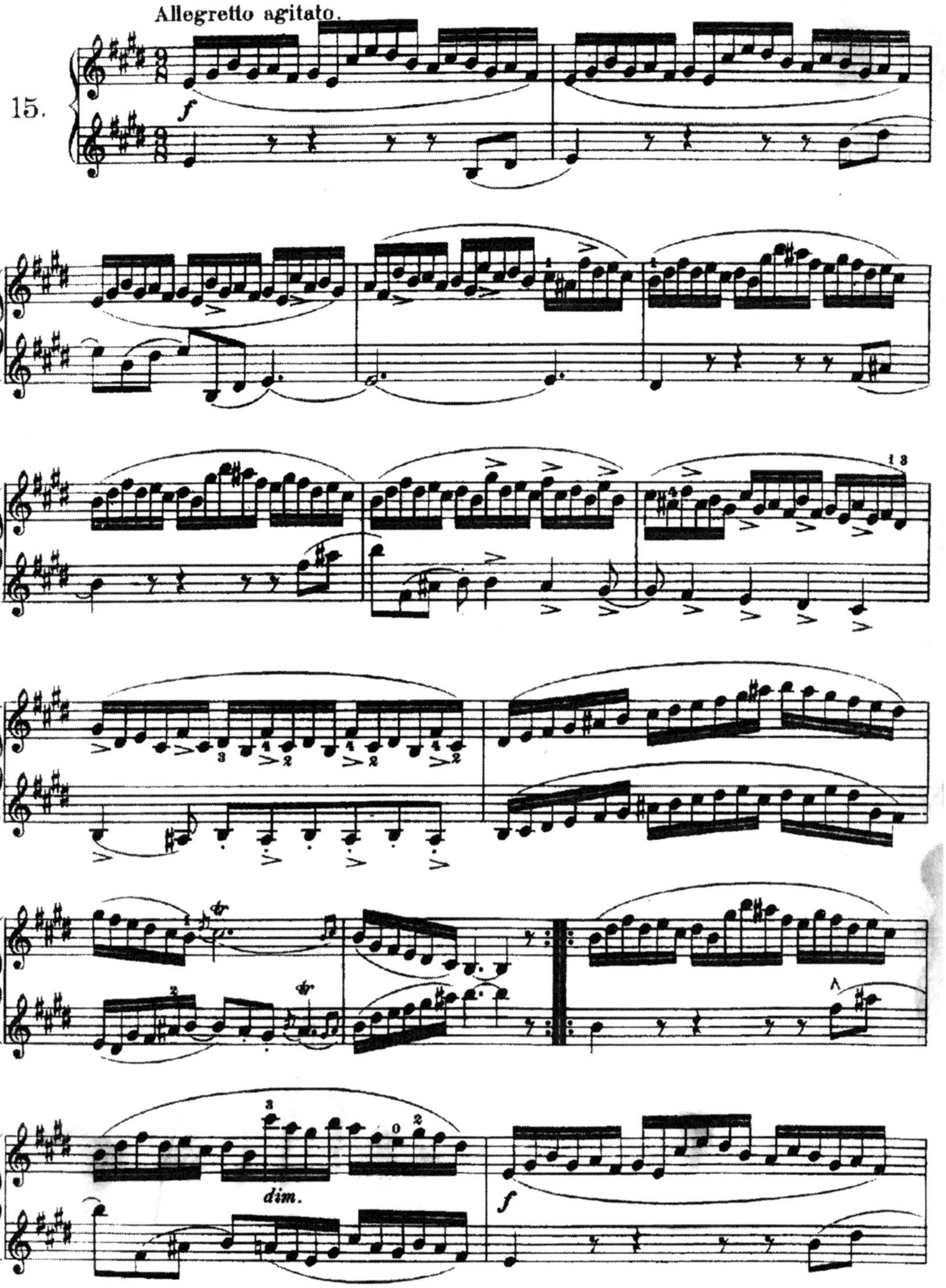

30

Allegretto agitato.

15.

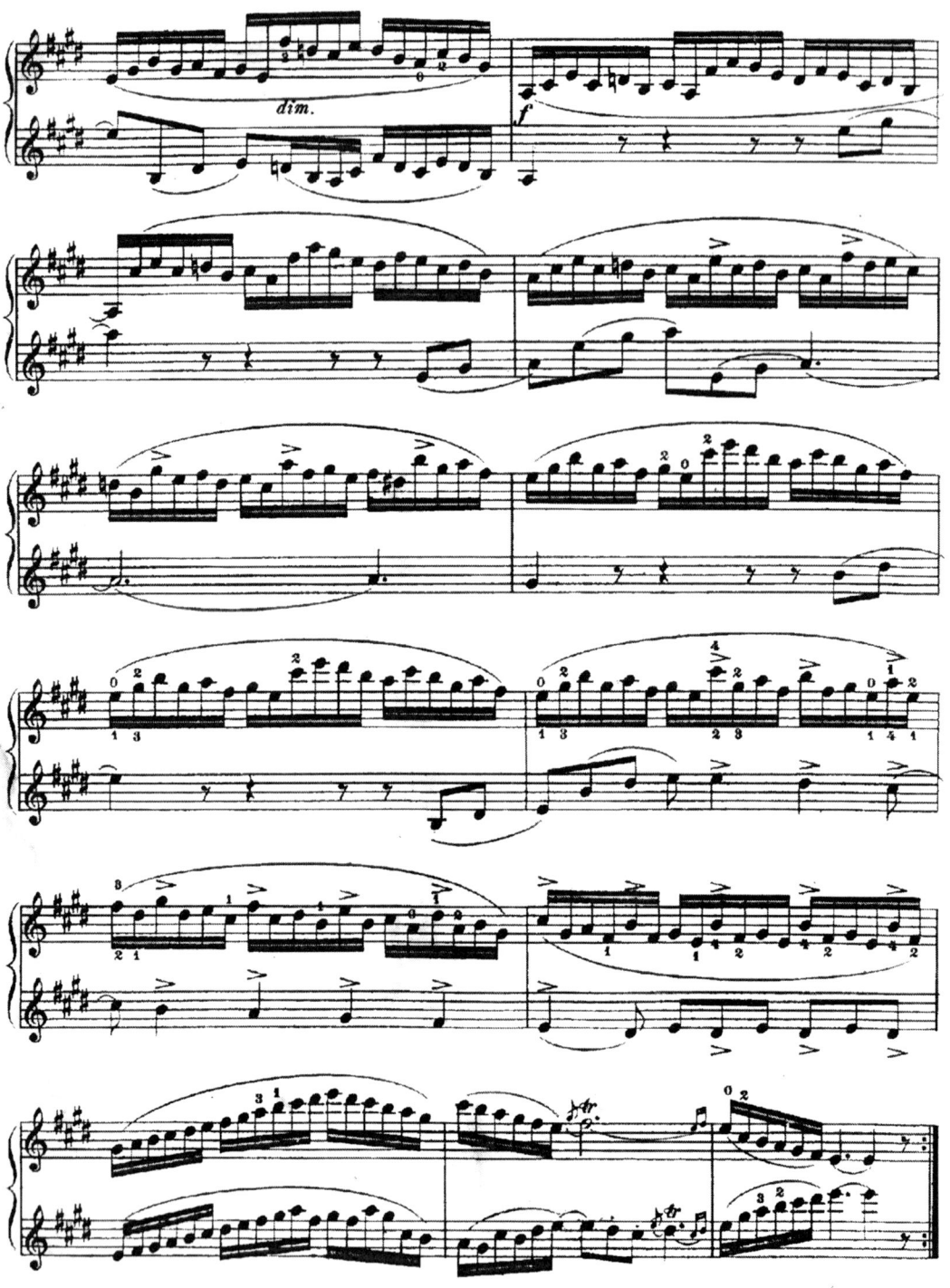

Allegretto spiccato.

17.

18243

Allegro ma non troppo.

18.

Vivace.

19.

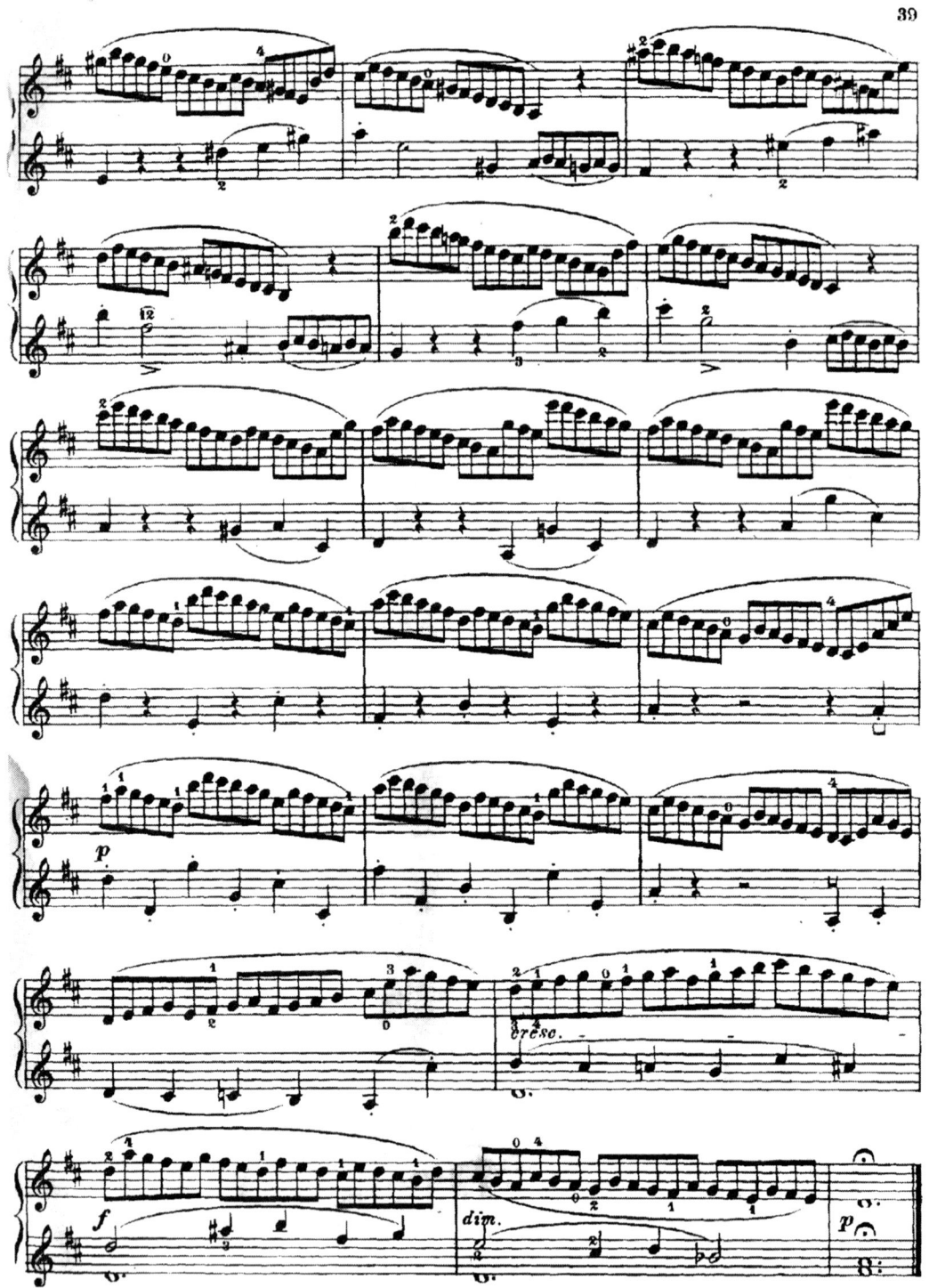

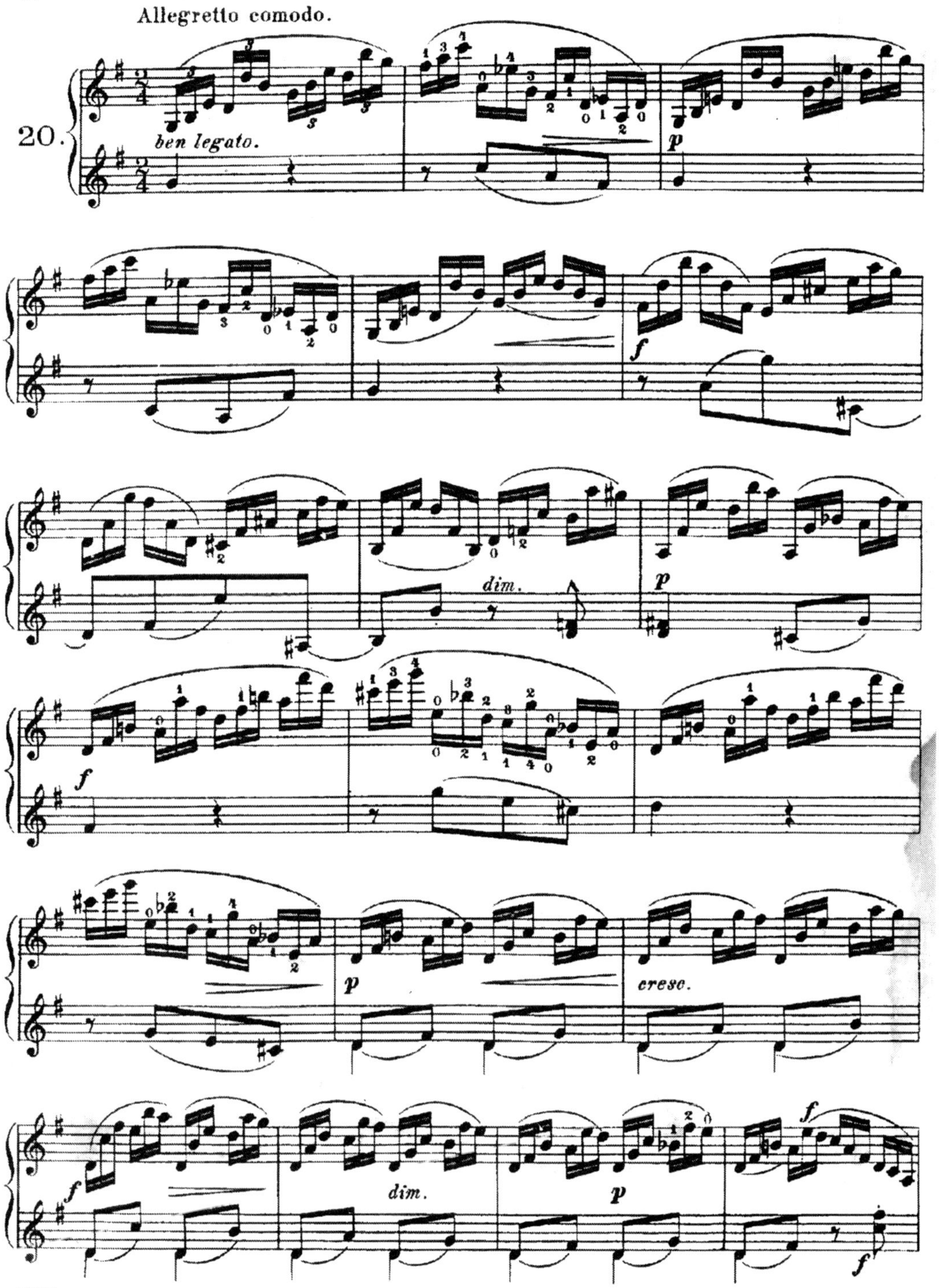
Allegretto comodo.
20.
ben legato.
dim.
cresc.
dim.

SCHIRMER'S SCHOLASTIC SERIES

Material for Vocal and Instrumental Study—"from the very easiest to the most difficult"

(The Numbers listed below cover Study-Material for Instruments other than Piano)

A Complete Catalog of Schirmer's Scholastic Series will be mailed upon request

G. SCHIRMER, Inc., NEW YORK

A 557

SCHIRMER'S LIBRARY
of MUSICAL CLASSICS
COMPOSITIONS FOR VIOLIN

In ordering please mention Schirmer's Library and give number
Complete Catalog of Schirmer's Library mailed free upon request

A 573   **Published by**   **G. SCHIRMER**   **New York**

CPSIA information can be obtained at www.ICGtesting.com
Printed in the USA
LVOW111016210113

316538LV00005B/296/P